TELL ME ABOUT

THE WORLD OF
ANIMALS

SERIES EDITOR: JACKIE GAFF
ILLUSTRATED BY ERIC ROBSON

Kingfisher Books

Series editor: Jackie Gaff
Series designer: Terry Woodley
Author: Tom Stacy
Designer: Camilla Hughes
Cover illustration: Bernard Long (Temple Rogers)
Editor: Stella Maidmont
Editorial assistant: Anne O'Daly

Kingfisher Books, Grisewood & Dempsey Ltd, Elsley House,
24–30 Great Titchfield Street, London W1P 7AD

First published in paperback in 1992 by Kingfisher Books
10 9 8 7 6 5 4 3
Originally published in hardback in 1990 by Kingfisher Books
Copyright © Grisewood & Dempsey Ltd 1990

BRITISH LIBRARY CATALOGUING IN PUBLICATION DATA
A catalogue record for this book is available from the
British Library

ISBN 0 86272 613 1

Phototypeset by Southern Positives and Negatives
(SPAN), Lingfield, Surrey
Printed and bound in Spain

Contents

What are animals like?

There are thousands of different animals in the world, but they all have one thing in common. They have to move about in order to find food and water. Unlike plants, animals cannot stay in one place and still remain alive. Some animals look for plants to eat, while others hunt and kill other animals. But whether they have legs, wings or fins, animals have to search for food.

In the northern forests, owls fly silently at night, hunting small animals to eat.

Forest deer graze on grass, bark and leaves. Only the males have antlers.

The stealthy lynx hunts small animals. Like all cats, it has very keen eyesight.

Bears catch fish in the rivers. On land they look for fruit and berries to eat.

The otter lives in a river-bank den. It can swim fast, which helps it to catch fish.

Woodpeckers use their powerful beaks to drill into tree bark in search of insects.

The porcupine chews pine-tree bark. Its spiny quills protect it from enemies.

The squirrel uses its sharp teeth to gnaw nuts. It buries some food for winter.

Raccoons eat crabs, frogs, fish, birds' eggs, insects, plants – almost anything!

 ## ANIMAL FACTS

- The animal world is divided into two main groups – vertebrates and invertebrates. Vertebrates are animals with backbones. This group includes all the really big animals, as well as many smaller creatures such as mice.

Backbone

RABBIT

- Invertebrates are animals that don't have backbones – insects such as flies, as well as worms and jellyfish.

JELLYFISH

- Experts have named nearly 1.3 million animals. About 96% are invertebrates. Just under 4% are vertebrates.

- There are five main vertebrate groups – fish, amphibians, reptiles, birds and mammals.

- There are around 22,000 species, or kinds, of fish.

- Amphibians can live on land and in water. There are over 4000 species, and they include frogs and toads.

- Snakes, lizards and crocodiles are all reptiles. There are over 6500 species and most live on land.

- There are just over 9000 bird species, of all shapes, sizes and colours.

- Mammals are the only animals whose young feed on the mother's milk. Familiar animals such as cats belong to this group, as well as lions and bears. There are over 4000 species.

Where do animals live?

Animals live in every part of the Earth — on land, in the ocean, and in the air. The area surrounding an animal's home is called its habitat. There are different habitats all over our planet, with different kinds of animals living in each one.

GREENLAND

NORTH AMERICA

Animals of the icy North, such as polar bears, have thick coats or layers of fat to keep them warm.

AFRICA

SOUTH AMERICA

Some animals of the prairies graze on its short grasses. Some hunt and kill other animals for their food.

Deserts are hot and very dry. Camels and other desert animals have to survive with little or no water to drink.

Rainforests are hot and wet. Many animals sleep in the day and hunt in the cool of the night.

Shy animals like badgers, owls and deer live hidden in the cool dark forests of northern Europe.

EUROPE

? DO YOU KNOW

Animals have all sorts of ways of surviving the different habitats in which they live. Desert animals have to manage with very little water, for example. Some never drink, and get all the water they need from their food instead. Others can live for long periods of time on the water stored in their body fat.

The deep oceans are rich in animal life of all shapes and sizes, from jellyfish to octopuses and sharks.

ASIA

Australia is home to unusual animals such as the emu, the kangaroo, the platypus and the koala.

AUSTRALIA

Lions are the big hunters of the African plains. The rhinoceros and the antelope are grass-eaters.

The icy coastal waters of Antarctica are the habitat of seals and whales, as well as penguins and other seabirds.

ANTARCTICA

Which animal lives the longest?

The longest living animals are tortoises — some live to be over 150 years old! Because they face many dangers, wild animals don't usually live as long as pets or zoo animals. And, as a rule, big animals live longer than small ones like insects.

Adult mayflies live for only a few hours.

A butterfly can live for up to a year.

Houseflies live for 2 to 3 months.

Mice may live for as long as 1 year in the wild, but up to 6 years as pets.

Hamsters usually live for 18–24 months.

A dog is very old at 15 years.

Horses can live to be 40 years old.

Cockatoos live for as long as 75 years.

Some giant tortoises live to be over 150.

SNAIL WATCHING

Garden snails live for 2 to 3 years, but you needn't spend that long watching them! Mark a snail's shell with a felt-tip pen. See where it goes and which plants it eats.

Which is the cleverest animal?

Animal intelligence is hard to measure, but most experts think that chimpanzees and dolphins come top of the class. Chimpanzees can use simple tools, while dolphins talk to one another under water, using a musical language of their own.

Chimpanzees use sticks as tools to 'fish' termites from their nests. Dolphins are playful and can easily be trained to perform tricks.

Which is the most dangerous animal?

Although a few types of shark will attack swimmers, the deadliest animals are smaller. Some snakes, spiders and jellyfish have poisonous bites or stings which can kill a person in minutes. The frog shown below has enough poison to kill 500 people!

? DO YOU KNOW

As many as 40,000 people a year die from snake bites. Most of these deaths take place in India and neighbouring countries.

Although tiny, the golden arrow-poison frog is even more deadly than the great white shark.

The saw-edged teeth of the great white shark can be 7.5 cm long.

What are the fastest animals?

The slowest mammal is the three-toed sloth. It sleeps for 16 hours out of every 24, and takes a whole day to travel just 100 metres!

Birds are the record-holders for speed. In a dive, a peregrine falcon can reach 300 km/h – only the fastest racing cars could beat it! In level flight another bird, the common eider duck, can fly at speeds of more than 76 km/h. The champion sprinter of all the land animals is the cheetah. But in a race it would just be beaten by a fish – the sailfish.

| km/h | 1 | 10 | 20 | 30 | 40 | 50 | 60 | 70 |

DO YOU KNOW

The champion long-distance traveller is a seabird called the Arctic tern. It nests in the Arctic, near to the North Pole. When summer ends there, it flies to the Antarctic, where summer is just beginning. Each year the amazing Arctic tern travels up to 36,000 km on its round trip across the world!

SPEED FACTS

	km/h
Peregrine falcon	300+
Sailfish	110
Cheetah	100+
Pronghorn	96
Gazelle	80
Eider duck	76
Hare	72
Racehorse	70
Ostrich	64
Greyhound	64
Fox	64
Zebra	64
Shark	64
Kangaroo	64
Lion	58
Dragonfly	58
Giraffe	51
Cat	48
Elephant	40
Sea lion	40
Dolphin	40
Human	32
Bat	24
Pig	18
Honeybee	18
Chicken	14
Housefly	8
Goldfish	6
Snake	3
Spider	2
Tortoise	0.4
Sloth	0.1
Snail	0.05

3 The pronghorn antelope can run at 64 km/h for about 3 km, and sprint at 96 km/h over short disances.

2 The cheetah can sprint at over 100 km/h when hunting, but it tires very quickly.

1 The sailfish is the world's fastest fish. In a test, one reached 110 km/h.

80   90   100   110   120   130   140   150   160

What are the largest animals?

Whales are the largest animals on Earth. And the biggest whale is the blue whale, which can be 30 metres long and weigh as much as 150 tonnes. The largest land animal is the African elephant, which is twice as tall as a person and can weigh 7 tonnes.

? DO YOU KNOW

Some animals are called Goliath after a giant in the Bible. The Goliath beetle is the size of a man's fist. The Goliath spider is as big as this page!

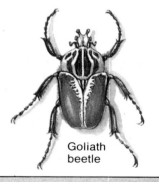

Goliath beetle

The tallest animal is the giraffe (5.5 metres). African elephants are the biggest plant-eaters (3.5 metres), while the largest meat-eater is the Kodiak bear (3 metres). The ostrich is the biggest bird (2.5 metres high). The longest snakes are the reticulated python and the anaconda (10 metres).

The blue whale is not a fish, but a mammal – its young feed on their mother's milk.

DO YOU KNOW

It would take about 22 African elephants (each weighing 7 tonnes) to balance the weight of just one blue whale! Even though the blue whale can weigh a staggering 150 tonnes, it lives on tiny shrimps called krill, which are only about 5 cm long. A blue whale may eat as much as 3 or 4 tonnes of krill every day.

The giant squid can be 17 metres long from its tentacles to the end of its body.

The largest fish is the harmless whale shark. It grows to 15 metres long.

Why do elephants have trunks?

As well as a nose to breathe through, an elephant's trunk is a hand for picking things up. It's long enough to reach up into tree tops for leaves, or down into pools for water. An elephant can even use its trunk like a hose to spray itself with water.

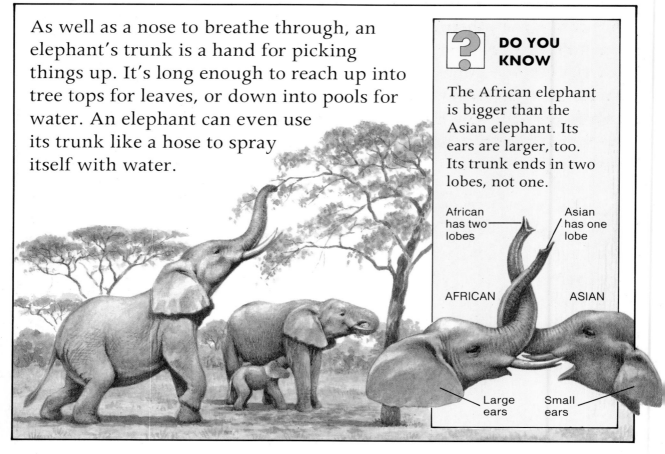

African has two lobes

Asian has one lobe

AFRICAN

ASIAN

Large ears

Small ears

Why are giraffes' necks so long?

With its long neck, a giraffe can reach even higher than an elephant's trunk to eat the juiciest leaves at the tops of trees.

The giraffe's extra-long neck has just seven bones – the same number as we have in ours!

Why do camels have humps?

A camel's hump helps it to survive life in the desert, where food and water are often scarce. When a camel has plenty to eat, its hump becomes firm with extra fat. The camel can then go without food or water for weeks, living off the emergency supplies in its hump.

DO YOU KNOW

There are two kinds of camel. The Arabian camel has just one hump. The Bactrian camel of central Asia has two humps.

Why do zebras have stripes?

No one knows why zebras have stripes. They may make it easier for zebras to see each other and stay together. They might also help to confuse enemies, making it difficult to pick out a single zebra from a galloping herd.

DO YOU KNOW

A tiger's stripes help it to hide by blending it into the shadows and long grasses.

Why do animals hibernate?

Hibernation is like a deep sleep, which some animals go into when food is scarce. In late summer, for example, the dormouse crams itself with fruit and nuts until it is very fat. Then it curls up inside its nest and goes to sleep. The dormouse lives off its body fat throughout the winter and wakes up in spring – thin and very hungry!

One type of Australian desert frog only comes out of hibernation after rain. It then lays its eggs in shallow pools, and its young grow into frogs before the pools dry out. Then each frog burrows into the sand, wrapping itself in a see-through skin to keep in body water. It may wait 2 years for the next rain.

Many hibernators are insect-eaters, like the hedgehog in its nest of dead leaves.

Snakes become sluggish in cold weather. They begin to stir only when it gets warmer.

Bats cluster together for winter, sleeping upside down in caves and old buildings.

Bears don't sleep deeply all winter. They wake on warm days to look for food to eat.

Chipmunks store food in their burrows. They wake on warm winter days to eat from their supplies.

The dormouse sleeps soundly in its nest until spring brings fresh plant food for it to eat.

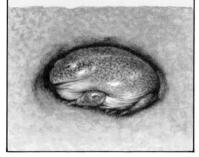

Why do kangaroos have pouches?

A kangaroo mother protects her baby in her pouch for the first few months of its life. A baby kangaroo is only a few millimetres long when it crawls into the pouch. It stays there, feeding on its mother's milk, until it is big enough to survive in the world outside. Animals that raise their young in pouches are called marsupials.

 MARSUPIAL FACTS

● There are around 270 marsupial species. The Americas are home to about 90.

● Australia has 180 or so types of marsupial, including kangaroos, koalas and wombats.

Kangaroos spring along on their big, powerful hind legs. Their long tails help them to balance.

NATURE DETECTIVE

Look for clues to show that animals have been feeding nearby. Look at nuts for animals' toothmarks, for example, and see if you can find any trees stripped of their bark by animals such as grazing deer.

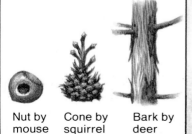

Nut by mouse   Cone by squirrel   Bark by deer

Why do chameleons change colour?

Chameleons are a type of lizard, whose skin colour changes with their mood – an angry chameleon will turn black! Chameleons are also affected by light and temperature, and their skins change slowly to match the colours of their surroundings.

Why do lizards lose their tails?

Most lizards can shed their tails when they want to. They often do this to get away from enemies, who are left clutching a wriggling bit of tail while the lizard escapes! The lizard's tail grows back again, but it's slightly shorter than before.

The hawk is left with only a wriggling tail in its talons, while the lizard escapes to grow a new tail.
   Animals like hawks which hunt and kill other animals for food are called predators.

Why do animals have shells?

All sorts of animals have shells, from crabs and lobsters to tortoises and turtles. Most of them have soft bodies, and their shells act rather like armour, protecting them from enemies. A tortoise, for example, can hide inside its shell if danger threatens.

 DO YOU KNOW

Tortoises (left) are land animals. Turtles (below) live in water and have paddle-like legs for swimming. Their shells are flatter than those of tortoises.

How do crocodiles hunt?

A crocodile will often lie in wait for animals that come to drink at the river's edge. It floats like a log, showing only its eyes and nostrils above water. If an animal strays too close, the crocodile grabs it and drags it under water until it drowns.

DO YOU KNOW

Crocodiles have narrower jaws than alligators, and the fourth tooth in a crocodile's lower jaw sticks out.

Alligator

Crocodile

How do birds fly?

Birds have two ways of flying – they glide with their wings outstretched, or they flap their wings up and down. Some birds use both methods. Small birds beat their wings very fast, while large birds tend to make slow wingbeats.

Birds have light bones and powerful muscles to help them fly. Their feathers keep them warm and make a smooth surface for the air to flow over in flight.

The frigatebird (below) has long pointed wings and a forked tail. It is a superb flier.

On broad wings over 3 metres across, the condor (above) soars on warm air currents above the mountains.

MAKE A BIRD MOBILE

1 Draw a body and two wings for each bird on stiff card. Colour them in and cut them out. Now fold the ends of each wing and staple them to the bodies.

2 Ask an adult to make a frame from two wire coat hangers.

3 Weight each bird with modelling clay. Tie the finished birds to the frame. Use different lengths of string so the birds don't bump into each other.

Fold wing and staple to body

The kestrel (left) hovers as it hunts. Wings beating and tail spread, it waits in the sky.

The albatross (above) is a glider, with the biggest wingspan of all birds – nearly 4 metres across!

Swifts (left) are very fast fliers. Their wings are swept back, like the wings of jet planes.

DO YOU KNOW

Not all birds can fly. Flightless birds include the largest living birds – the ostrich and the emu. Kiwis are shy flightless birds which live in New Zealand. They wander about on the ground at night, hunting for a juicy meal of insects and worms.

Penguins can't fly, but they can swim well. They use their wings as flippers in the water.

Emu

Kiwi

Emperor penguins

How do bats fly?

Bats fly by flapping their wings, just like birds do. Bats are mammals, however, not birds. Bats don't have feathers and their wings are covered in skin. A bat's wings are like a tent of thin skin, which stretches from the tips of the bat's fingerbones down to its feet and across to its tail.

Bats sleep in the day, roosting upside down in trees or caves. They wake at dusk.

Most bats see quite well, but their large ears help them to track insects when hunting at night.

 BAT FACTS

- The biggest bats are called flying foxes. Their wings can be 1.5 metres across.

- The smallest bat is Kitti's hog-nosed bat – it's no bigger than a bumblebee.

DO YOU KNOW

Some bats find insects in the dark by echolocation – sending out a stream of noise and measuring how far away an insect is by the time it takes the noise to reach it and bounce back off its body.

Bat sends out high-pitched squeaks

Echo bounces off insect

Can fish fly?

Fish can't really fly, but some can glide above the water to escape their enemies. Flying fish have extra-long shoulder fins which spread like wings. Once airborne, they can glide for more than 100 metres.

Can frogs fly?

Tree frogs are expert climbers, and some species will leap into the air to catch insects to eat. They can glide easily from tree to tree, and some tree frogs have large webbed feet which act rather like parachutes.

Tree frogs have pads on their fingers and toes which help them to climb trees.

How do fish swim?

Fish swim by waving or rippling their bodies along. The fish tightens the muscles down the side of its body – one side after the other – and this makes it ripple through the water. Its tail also helps, by pushing against the water behind it.

The fin on top of a fish's back is called its dorsal fin. The fish uses this fin to help it change direction.

The tail wiggles from side to side, helping to push the fish through the water.

The fish uses these fins – its pelvic fins – to keep its balance as it swims along.

To swim, the fish tightens the muscles down each side of its body – one side after the other. This sets up a rippling movement which pushes the fish through the water.

 DO YOU KNOW

The seahorse swims slowly in an upright position, by fanning its small dorsal fin so quickly that it looks like a boat's propeller.

MAKE AN AQUARIUM

1 You'll need a fish tank or a large glass container. Put in a layer of washed gravel and fill the tank slowly with clean water.

2 Plant some water-weed and add a broken flowerpot for your fish to hide in.

3 Let the tank stand for 3 days before you put in the fish. Don't over-crowd them – one small fish needs as much as 4 litres of water.

24

How do fish breathe under water?

All animals need to breathe oxygen to live. Unlike land animals, which take oxygen from the air, fish take it from the water in which they live. They have special body parts called gills inside them, which take the oxygen they need from the water.

To breathe, a fish gulps in water and passes it through its gills, where oxygen is absorbed into its bloodstream.

Hundreds of different colourful fish live in the warm shallow waters around coral reefs.

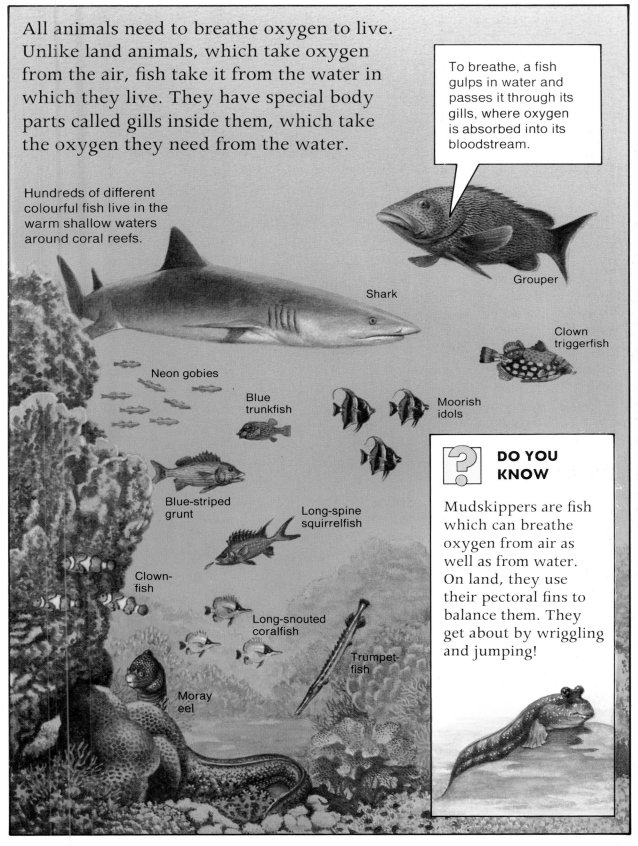

Grouper

Shark

Clown triggerfish

Neon gobies

Blue trunkfish

Moorish idols

Blue-striped grunt

Long-spine squirrelfish

Clown-fish

Long-snouted coralfish

Trumpet-fish

Moray eel

DO YOU KNOW

Mudskippers are fish which can breathe oxygen from air as well as from water. On land, they use their pectoral fins to balance them. They get about by wriggling and jumping!

Are all snakes poisonous?

Few snakes are poisonous. Some snakes kill animals for food by crushing them in their jaws. Others coil their long bodies around their victims and squeeze them to death. Out of about 3000 different snake species, only 300 or so use the needle-sharp fangs in their jaws to inject a deadly poison.

The reticulated python (below) – all pythons squeeze their victims to death.

The Australian taipan (below) is one of the world's most poisonous snakes.

The king cobra (left) rears up when frightened. All cobras have poison fangs.

 SNAKE FACTS

• Snakes can swallow animals wider than themselves. They open their mouths really wide by un-hinging their jaws.

• The reticulated python grows to 10 metres and uses its long and powerful body to squeeze its victims to death. It can even kill pigs and deer.

• Vipers have the longest poison fangs of all snakes – some have fangs as long as 5 cm!

Anacondas (below) rarely go far from water. They drown their victims or squeeze them to death.

Rattlesnakes (right) are very poisonous. They rattle the ends of their tails as a warning signal.

How do snakes move?

Even though they don't have legs, some snakes can move quicker than you can walk. Snakes have very strong muscles which they can tighten and relax to ripple or throw their bodies along. Some also dig the broad scales beneath their bodies into the ground, and then push against these 'anchors'.

1 Most snakes use their muscular bodies to ripple over stony ground, pushing against stones and other objects.

2 Most sidewinding snakes live in deserts. To move, this snake anchors its head and tail, then flings its middle sideways.

3 On smoother ground a snake may concertina its body, anchor its tail, then throw its head forwards.

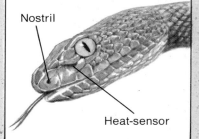

Nostril

Heat-sensor

1

2

3

How do tadpoles become frogs?

Tadpoles are more like tiny fish than frogs. They live in water, where they swim around breathing through gills. Tadpoles develop legs as they change into frogs, however. They also lose their gills and grow lungs for breathing on land.

1 Try watching tadpoles grow into frogs for yourself! Collect a little frogspawn from a pond in spring.

2 Put it in a bowl with some pond water and weed. Start a diary, to record all the changes as they take place.

1 Frogs lay jelly-like clumps of spawn, or eggs, in water.

4 Then they grow two front legs. Their tails shrink away and they develop lungs.

2 Each egg grows into a tiny tadpole, which breathes through gills.

3 You should see some tiny tadpoles after about 10 days. They'll get their food from the weed at first. When their legs begin to grow, give your tadpoles fish food to eat.

3 After a few weeks the tadpoles grow two back legs.

4 When all their legs have grown, put a stone in the bowl so the froglets can hop out of the water to breathe air. When they lose their tails, it's time to take your baby frogs back to their pond.

? DO YOU KNOW

Animals which live on land and in water are called amphibians. Even though most adult amphibians have lungs for breathing on land, they can't live far from water. This is because their skins are slimy and have to be kept fairly damp.

How can you tell frogs from toads?

There's very little difference between most frogs and toads, and it's often difficult to tell them apart. However, frogs tend to hop and leap about on land, while toads generally have shorter back legs and prefer to crawl. European frogs have smooth skins, while toads' skins are rather warty.

DO YOU KNOW

The record for a frog leap is over 6.5 metres, by a bullfrog.

AMPHIBIAN FACTS

● The Goliath frog of Africa is the world's largest frog. It can grow to nearly 37 cm – that's almost the width of two spread pages of this book – and weigh 3.5 kg!

● The largest amphibians are the giant salamanders of China and Japan. They sometimes grow to be more than 1.5 metres from head to tail tip.

● Unlike frogs and toads, salamanders (below) never lose their tails. They have small legs and move about on land with short clumsy steps.

Male frogs (right) blow up their throats with air when calling to attract a mate.

Most toads (below) have warty skins. The warts of some toads can be poisonous.

How do caterpillars become butterflies?

 DO YOU KNOW

Moths are related to butterflies. You can tell the difference between them by their wings. A butterfly holds its wings up over its back when resting. A moth folds its flat over its body.

BUTTERFLY

Knobbed antennae

MOTH

Hair-like antennae

WATCHING BUTTERFLIES

Learn about butterflies by watching them, not catching them. In summer, look for different kinds of butterfly. See which flowers they feed on, and look on leaves for eggs and caterpillars. Find out which garden flowers attract butterflies and see if you can grow some.

Every butterfly goes through four very different stages in its life-cycle. It starts as an egg, which then hatches into a caterpillar. Next it turns into a pupa, after which it finally becomes an adult. This life-cycle can take a few weeks or two years.

1 The life-cycle of a butterfly begins when a female lays her eggs on a plant. A hungry caterpillar hatches from each egg.

2 The caterpillar spends most of its time eating. It crawls around, chewing on leaves, and grows quickly.

4 The adult butterfly forms inside the pupa. When it is ready, it splits the pupa case open and crawls out.

3 When the caterpillar is fully grown, it turns into a pupa. It doesn't eat and it looks dead.

BUTTERFLY & MOTH FACTS

● The biggest butterflies are the birdwings of South-East Asia (below), with wingspans of 25–28 cm. Measure this against your hands!

● The largest moth is the ghost moth (below) from Central and South America. It measures more than 30 cm across.

● Other giant moths are the Atlas moth of India and the Hercules moth of Australia. Both measure about 25 cm across.

How do spiders spin webs?

Spiders spin their webs with two sorts of silk, which they make inside their bodies. One is a tough silk for the web's frame. The other is stretchy and sticky, and is used by the spider to weave its main insect trap.

1 The spider begins by spinning a bridge of tough silk, which it makes inside its body.

2 Then it pulls down a thread to make a triangle-shape.

3 It adds more tough threads to complete the frame, first from the centre and then around the middle.

4 Finally, the spider fills the frame in with stretchy silk. It bites and kills insects caught in its sticky trap.

TRAPPING MINIBEASTS

Here's a way to trap small creatures so that you can study them without harming them.

1 Bury a glass jar outdoors. Place a lid on stones, to stop it filling with water if it rains.

2 Check your trap each morning to see what you've caught. Try to find the creatures' names in a guide book, then let them go.

3 Put traps in wet and dry places, to see whether you catch the same kinds of creatures in each habitat.

Are spiders insects?

Although you might think spiders look rather like beetles and other crawling insects, they belong to a separate animal group called the arachnids. The main difference between the two groups is that insects have six legs, while arachnids such as spiders and scorpions have eight.

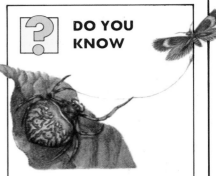

? DO YOU KNOW

The bolas spider gets its name from the weighted rope used as a lasso by South American cowboys. It spins a single thread of silk with a sticky blob at the end, and swings it to catch flying insects.

 INSECT FACTS

● Experts have named over 950,000 insects. Several thousand more are named every year.

● Ants and bees are related. They often live in large groups called colonies.

● Beetles have hard cases to cover and protect their wings. This is a stag beetle.

● Dragonflies are fast fliers – they have been recorded reaching speeds of 58 km/h!

● Flies have one pair of flying wings. Their knobbly back ones help with balance.

● Bugs range in size from tiny aphids 2 mm long (above), to giants of 110 mm!

● Butterflies and moths feed on the nectar of flowers, sipping it through special mouth-parts called proboscises.

● Grasshoppers are jumpers, with strong back legs. They fly with their back wings.

How do bees make honey?

Bees make honey from nectar, the sugary liquid that they collect from flowers. Back in the hive, the bees mix the nectar with a special substance from their bodies to turn it into honey. They store the honey in little wax 'rooms' called cells. The cells are hexagonal, or six-sided, and the honeycomb is formed from them. The bees eat the honey in the winter.

 BEE FACTS

• Large bee hives may have 60,000 worker bees in them, but only one queen.

• It takes the life's work of ten bees to fill one 450-gram pot of honey.

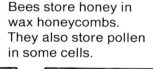 Bees store honey in wax honeycombs. They also store pollen in some cells.

 TEST INSECT TASTES

Try this outdoors on a warm summer's day, when there are lots of insects about. Don't get too close, though, as some insects will sting if disturbed. You'll need four small dishes and some coloured paper.

1 Stand each dish on a square of coloured paper. Put milk in one dish, sugary water in the 2nd, salty water in the 3rd, and jam in the 4th. Label the paper for each different food.

2 Wait to see which insects come to feed. Note which ones visit each dish. Count how many insects feed in half an hour and see which food attracts the most insects to it.

Sugar   Salt   Jam   Milk

Why do bees and wasps sting?

A worker honeybee stings to defend its hive. It can only use its sting once, then it dies. Queen bees fight each other, though, and can sting more than once. Wasps can also sting several times. They use their stings to stun or kill other insects, as well as to defend their nests.

A bee sting (below) is a barbed tube, which hooks tightly in place while poison is pumped down it.

How do flies walk upside down?

Flies have special hooks and sucker pads on their feet (left) which help them walk upside down.

Flies can walk up windows and across ceilings because they have special hooks and sucker pads on their feet instead of toes. These can grip even the smoothest surface. Houseflies like the insect above have two hooked claws and two sticky sucker pads on each foot.

FLY FACTS

● The buzzing of a fly is the sound of its wings beating at over 100 times a second.

When did dinosaurs live?

None of our human ancestors ever saw a live dinosaur. This is because dinosaurs died out 65 million years ago, long before human beings appeared on Earth. We have learnt about dinosaurs by studying their fossils – bones and other body remains which over the centuries have turned to stone. This is how we know that the dinosaur age started 225 million years ago and continued for about 160 million years.

The pterosaurs weren't dinosaurs, but they lived at the same time. They also died out about 65 million years ago.

Corythosaurus was a plant-eating dinosaur, about 10 metres long, with a duck-like bill and a crest on its head.

Brachiosaurus was a gigantic 23 metres long! Its long neck helped it to browse at the top of the tallest plants.

Stegosaurus moved slowly but was heavily armoured, with bony plates on its back and a spiked tail.

At 12 metres high, Brachiosaurus was the tallest of all the dinosaurs. If it were alive today it would easily be able to peer over our rooftops. Its long neck only had 14 bones in it, and each bone was nearly half a metre long!

Tyrannosaurus was one of the largest meat-eaters ever. It was 15 metres long and had large sharp teeth up to 18 cm long.

Ornitholestes was the size of a dog. It was a meat-eating hunter and could run swiftly on its long back legs.

Triceratops was about 9 metres long. It had a huge armoured head, with three horns for fighting off enemies.

Why do animals become extinct?

One of the main reasons why animals become extinct, or die out, is because a major change takes place in their habitat – the weather becomes too cold or too hot, for example, or the plants or animals on which they feed are hard to find. Nowadays, these changes are often brought about by people. Even bulldozing a small wood to make way for a new housing estate can cause some of the animals that lived there to become extinct.

The survival of the gentle gorilla is now threatened, as more and more of its forest habitat is destroyed.

DANGER FACTS

● More than 300 mammal and bird species have died out since the 1600s. In that time, the number of human beings has increased from 580 million to about 5500 million.

● Thousands of animals are now on the danger list – from tiny insects like the butterfly below, to giants like the African elephant and the blue whale.

Regal fritillary

Javan rhino

● There are only about 50 Javan rhinos left in the world.

● Experts think that unless habitats are better protected, we may lose as many as 15 mammal, 30 bird, 90 fish and over 2000 insect species every single year.

Useful words

Amphibian   One of the main groups of vertebrate animals. Amphibians live on land and in water, and they include frogs and toads, salamanders and newts. Most amphibians have damp, slimy skin and lay jelly-like eggs.

Backbone   Another word for spine – the row of bones which runs down the back of humans and all other vertebrate animals.

Gill   A body part for breathing oxygen from water. Fish have gills for breathing under water.

Habitat   The area surrounding an animal's home. It includes the weather and the plants that grow there, as well as the other animals that live there.

Hibernation   A type of deep sleep which can last several months. Some animals hibernate when there is very little food or water around, or when the weather is very cold. During this time the animals hardly ever wake up and they don't eat. Instead, they live off their own body fat.

Fly   Butterfly   Bee

Invertebrate   An animal which doesn't have a backbone. Jellyfish, worms, and insects such as flies and bees are all invertebrates. Some invertebrates, such as snails, have an outside shell to protect their soft bodies. There are over 1 million invertebrate species.

Lung   A body part for breathing oxygen from air. All mammals have lungs – even whales!

Mammal   An animal that feeds its young on milk from the mother's body. Mammals have lungs for breathing air.

Marsupial   A type of mammal, which raises its young in the mother's pouch. Kangaroos are marsupials, for example.

Reptile   One of the main groups of vertebrate animals. Snakes and lizards, crocodiles and alligators, turtles and tortoises are all reptiles. Unlike fish and amphibians, with their slimy skins and jelly-like eggs, most reptiles have dry scaly skin and the eggs they lay have leathery skins.

Species   A unique, or special, type of animal. Blue whales are one species within the whale group, for example. Other whale species are humpback whales and sperm whales.

Vertebrate   An animal with a backbone. The main groups of vertebrate are fish, amphibians, reptiles, birds and mammals. There are about 45,000 vertebrate species.

Index